my search *for the* Real Heaven
workbook

Steve Hemphill

my search *for the* Real Heaven workbook

TATE PUBLISHING
AND ENTERPRISES, LLC

My Search for the Real Heaven Workbook
Copyright © 2012 by Steve Hemphill. All rights reserved.

No part of this publication may be reproduced, stored in a retrieval system or transmitted in any way by any means, electronic, mechanical, photocopy, recording or otherwise without the prior permission of the author except as provided by USA copyright law.

The opinions expressed by the author are not necessarily those of Tate Publishing, LLC.

Published by Tate Publishing & Enterprises, LLC
127 E. Trade Center Terrace | Mustang, Oklahoma 73064 USA
1.888.361.9473 | www.tatepublishing.com

Tate Publishing is committed to excellence in the publishing industry. The company reflects the philosophy established by the founders, based on Psalm 68:11, *"The Lord gave the word and great was the company of those who published it."*

Book design copyright © 2012 by Tate Publishing, LLC. All rights reserved.
Cover design by Lance Waldrop
Interior design by Nathan Harmony

Published in the United States of America
ISBN: 978-1-62295-792-7
1. Religion / Christian Life / Death, Grief, Bereavement
2. Religion / Biblical Studies / General
12.09.06

Table of Contents

Preface	7
Chapter 1: Literal Versus Symbolic	17
Chapter 2: Prophecy Indications	29
Chapter 3: Satan's Strategy	47
Chapter 4: Purification by Fire	65
Chapter 5: Resurrection and Our New Body	83
Chapter 6: Connecting Eternity, Heaven, and New Earth	101
Chapter 7: God Promotes a Reward System	121
Chapter 8: Reunion	129

Preface

When *My Search for the Real Heaven* was released in 2009, I had no idea how my life was about to change. Although I had felt God's hand on me and on this project from the very beginning, I wasn't really prepared for all the things that were about to happen. It was truly like wandering through a waking dream.

I quickly began seeing and hearing wildly encouraging responses from people I didn't even know. One woman got a book from my mother, read it in two days, and quickly came back for ten more to share with her entire family. A lawyer heard me speak and ordered thirty copies to give to all his friends. An elderly lady returned on a Thursday evening for another one of my lectures, bringing her sixteen-year-old grandson who was visiting from another state for two weeks. She introduced me to the young man, and quickly told me she had asked him what he would like to do that evening. She was shocked when he said he wanted to, "go back and hear that man talk some more about heaven." Another petite elderly woman shuffled up to me and said, "Honey, I want you to know that for the first time in my forty years of going to church, you was through talkin' a'fore I was through listnin'." Wow. What a compliment.

I am shocked and humbled by these acts of kindness and many more. One of these that stands out the most was a message from a woman I had never met. A friend had given her a copy of my book as a gift, and she had stayed up all night reading every page. Her mother and sister had both died in a short two-week time span, and she had completely lost her appetite, her ability to sleep, and her love for life. "Thank you so much," she began, "for answering all my questions about heaven. Now I can sleep and eat again."

Another big surprise was how many people told me that they had just finished my book and were about to read it again. Again? I rarely read a book again, and if I do it's because I enjoyed it long ago. I never finish a book and start it over immediately. "Why?" I asked these people. Their answer was prompt, "I hurried through to get the whole picture. Now I plan to read it through again more slowly and look up the verses in my own Bible."

Especially shocking about all these testimonials was this important detail: I was untrained as far as ministry was concerned. Yes, I was college educated, but in the area of business and marketing. For this reason I kept asking, "Why me, Lord. Don't you have someone more qualified?"

As I pondered this important question, I realized that God often uses people in areas other that the ones they appear to be gifted in. Paul is one excellent example of this. As a highly educated Jew and a strict Pharisee, in my opinion he was a perfect choice to take the gospel of Jesus Christ to the Jewish people. But God had a much different plan. He sent Paul to the gentiles. Then it began to dawn on me. I know and love marketing—with a passion. What is more important to market with enthusiasm than eternity with God? Nothing. Maybe this all made sense after all.

Something else I slowly began to realize was that heaven was often ignored completely or covered only briefly in most Christian colleges, seminaries, and preacher training institutions. One recent graduate attended two of my lectures and ran to me afterward offering high praise and thanks. He quickly explained that as he was recently completing his education that equipped him to minister to others, he realized that no training at all had been offered about heaven. He had discussed this paradox with several of his graduating classmates, and they all decided to approach one of their favorite educators with this question. When they did so, this long-time, highly educated and esteemed professor responded with, "Heaven is better than the alternative." This young man's bitter disappointment came through, "That wasn't good enough for us. So I am especially thankful for your presentations and work. Now I am ready to find my place in ministry." "Thank You, God," I said in my heart. "Thank You for letting me be an inspiration to this man and others like him. Use me to Your glory. Bless many others through my story."

Another interesting and encouraging phenomenon began to happen as I began to speak around the country and offer a period of questions and answers at the end of each presentation. People began to ask many interesting and often very personal questions. Their frankness and openness was somewhat shocking, but quite encouraging at the same time. I always prayed before each presentation. I prayed for God to send the people He chose, and I prayed I would say the right words. When you study something for seven years, there are so many things to cover that you can go a variety of directions in any given presentation. I try to let God lead in each one, and no two presentations are exactly the same.

One Sunday evening in a small Northeast Texas community I answered this question: "Is it s sin to be cremated?" I always start with, "Well, God made you from dirt. I don't think it's any problem for Him to restore you from ashes—He is God!" Then I add, "Some were burned to death in horrible circumstances and had no choice, and since we know even the sea will give up its dead that have been eaten by marine life, these people won't miss out on the resurrection." Then I try to keep it light with this final comment, "Besides all that, cremation is much cheaper, and I am a tightwad, so I am seriously thinking about being cremated too." That always gets a chuckle.

After the question and answer session ended that evening, an older couple came up to me in tears thanking me for answering the cremation question. "You have no idea how much that meant to us," they began. "Our only child has cancer and was moved to hospice today, and we just discovered that his wife is planning on cremating him. We were very upset—even devastated by the news until tonight when you answered that question. Now we realize it doesn't matter. Thank you for covering that."

I learned the next morning that when they got home from my presentation they got a call from hospice and rushed to hold their son's hand as he died—just two hours later. Only God could coordinate events like that. I praise His holy name.

So here we are, ready to begin a small group study together on a most excellent topic: Heaven! I now offer this prayer on your behalf:

Lord, bless this study and this small group. Open their eyes and ears and heart and mind to the eternal truths You are ready to reveal. I pray this nurtures an eternal enthusiasm for our heavenly existence in such a profound way that these Christians will feel the fire in their bones to share it with many others and greatly enlarge the boarders of Your kingdom. In Jesus Name, Amen.

Going Deeper

Bookstores have two basic sections: fiction, and non-fiction. I did the unthinkable by mixing the two in one book. I tried to do it in a very gentle way, calling the section at the end of each chapter, "What Might Be." I did this to prevent offending anyone and to separate my search for biblical truth about heaven from my thoughts about what might be happening—based on the Bible revelations I was seeing.

These sections have been popular with readers, so this led me to include some thought questions and discussion questions about these sections as well as the non-fictional parts. I hope it encourages you to think deeper about heaven, as well as causing great anticipation about your eternal, heavenly home with the King.

Background

When my Dad died in the summer of 2000, I couldn't find any books on heaven at the Bible bookstore. This was a great shock to me. I asked, "If we are not excited about heaven, doesn't that sort of kill the spirit of evangelism?" So I bought a new Bible and prayed a new prayer:

Lord, I'm looking for heaven. Help me to find it. You know what you meant when You wrote this, so please help me to know what you mean as I read it. In Jesus Name, Amen.

It worked. I found all kinds of things in the Scriptures that I had never heard of. I also realized that although I had heard many sermons on "hell-fire and brimstone," I had never heard a sermon on heaven. Not a single one.

I believe that heaven was revealed to Christians (1 Corinthians 2:10) to motivate us toward evangelism. If you're not excited about where you're going, you aren't likely to take others with you there—and vice-versa.

So I am admitting right up front that my goal is to get you so excited about heaven that you become actively involved in helping take others with you there. Technically, it's called, "Personal Evangelism," but I really hate to use that term because it conjures up images of knocking the doors of mean people who are totally uninterested in hearing about your church. What I'm really talking about is the only kind of evangelism that really works: "Friendship Evangelism."

We all know people who live life without God; people who have no personal relationship with Jesus Christ. That's no way to live. It's lonely, depressing, and destined for failure.

I want to shake things up and offer an important Biblical truth: you can have a personal, daily, ongoing conversational relationship with God.

Abraham had a personal, ongoing, conversational relationship with God. Joseph, Moses, and David had personal, ongoing, conversational relationships with Him too. Noah, David, Daniel, and many other examples are listed in the scriptures. I think they are there for one purpose: to convince you that you can have the same thing.

God isn't called the great "I WAS." He is the great "I AM." He makes this very clear in Exodus 3:14. You can be a Bible story too. Begin today. Draw close to God, and He will draw close to you (James 4:8). He is your shield in times of trouble (Psalm 84:11), your deliverer in distress (Psalm 40:17), and your salvation in the end (Psalm 18:2). He invites you to lean on Him (Psalm 22:10) and let Him provide you some rest (Matthew 11:28). Accept that offer. Become His close friend.

Abraham was a friend of God (James 2:23). Jesus even told his disciples at the end of His ministry that they were no longer His disciples—they were His friends (John 15:15). Are you a friend of God? He saves His friends! Spend time in His love letter to you (the Bible).

Background Discussion Questions

What do you think heaven will be like? Describe and discuss it.

_____

_____

_____

_____

_____

Have you read any books on heaven? Which ones?

_____

_____

_____

_____

In reading about heaven in a book or in the Bible, what are the most surprising possibilities you have encountered?

_____

_____

_____

_____

Review

Read pages 22-23 in book

What Might Be: Arrival

Discussion Questions

1. Why call heaven the "real" world?
2. Do you think we really have an angelic escort when we die?
3. Are angels really assigned to help people on earth?
4. Is your heavenly home really built from your good deeds done on earth?
5. Do we really have a heavenly "account" where our good deeds are recorded?
6. Is there really a "reward ceremony" for Christians at the final judgment?
7. How are people "image-bearers" for God?

8. Are angels really servants for people who will end up in heaven?

9. Are angels really sometimes "reassigned"?

10. Are there really going to be parties and celebrations in heaven?

Home

After I left for college, things were never the same. For some, home spurs pleasant memories. For others, not so much. Satan wants you to remember your family—and especially your father—in a very unpleasant light. Why? Because if you don't trust, admire, or love your earthly father, it makes it much more difficult to do so with your heavenly one.

When you think of home, do you think of pleasant experiences, or unpleasant ones? Explain:

_____
_____
_____
_____
_____

List a few of your most vivid memories of home:

_____
_____
_____
_____

An Unattractive Heaven

What are the things about heaven that you are excited about and look forward to? Explain:

_____
_____
_____
_____

Do you pray for Jesus to return soon? If not, why not?

_____

Do you actually dread heaven? Why? Explain:

_____

_____

_____

_____

Many think we will be floating spirits on clouds playing the harp and worshiping twenty-four-seven. What do you think?

_____

_____

_____

_____

An inaccurate view of heaven hinders evangelism. You may not agree with every idea suggested here, but I hope you will honestly consider them, pray, and get excited about heaven! But remember, this is not a salvation issue.

The Christian Goal

Why do professional athletes endure hardship and discipline and training? Because they believe they can ultimately get a gold medal in front of a cheering crowd. What is the goal of Christians? Heaven. Yet heaven has not been discussed very much. Why?

_____

_____

_____

_____

Scriptural Authority

Where should you go for the truth about what heaven will be like?

_____

Who invented language?

_____

Is it possible the words in the Bible don't really mean what they say?

_____

Is it possible God accidentally used the wrong words in some places in the Bible?

_____

God invented language and all communication. Out of all the ways he could have revealed truth, he chose words. Is it safe to assume He chose the right ones? ☐ Yes ☐ No

Read 2 Timothy 3:16-17. Where does all Scripture originate? Is it trustworthy? Explain:

_____

_____

_____

_____

What is this Scripture teaching us about heaven?

_____

_____

_____

_____

(Read John 16:13) How is God involved with the discovery of truth? How can we really know about what our heavenly future will be like?

_____

_____

_____

_____

Beginning In Prayer

Lord, I pray that every person who wants to know about heaven will be given new insights. As we start this study, open our eyes, ears, hearts, and minds to the truth about our eternal future. Don't let Satan deceive us. Please reveal kingdom secrets as we study. In Jesus's name, Amen.

Review

Read pages 29-32 in book

What Might Be: The Five Earths of Scripture

Discussion Questions

1. Are there really books in heaven?
2. What is "new earth"? Is it real? Is it temporary, or eternal?
3. Was the original earth really perfect? Discuss.
4. Could the original earth really have been a part of heaven?
5. Was the original earth truly safe; completely void of dangers, thorns, death, or sickness?
6. Did God really walk and talk with Adam on the original earth?
7. Why doesn't God (in tangible form) have contact with our earth?
8. Why is there always fire when God visits earth after the curse (like Mt. Sinai)?
9. Was the original earth really "good"? Isn't everything physical evil?
10. Is there really going to be some sort of "purification fire" on earth someday?

11. How was the second earth, the cursed earth, different from the original earth?

12. Cain murdered Able during the time of the cursed earth—were there no murders on the original one?

13. Was Noah's family really the only good family on the cursed earth?

14. What did God mean when He said He would "destroy" the earth with a flood?

15. Of the five earths in Scripture, which one do we live on now?

16. What two earths are still in the future?

17. Why did the angel call the Bible a "guidebook"?

18. Won't we automatically and immediately know everything when we get to heaven?

Chapter 1: Literal Versus Symbolic

The Father of Oceanography

Matthew Maury is known as the father of oceanography. One day he read Psalm 8:6-8 and wondered if these paths in the sea were literal.

What does God reveal about the sea? Was it literal? Explain:

_____

Maury read this and went to discover them. He joined the U. S. Navy and became Superintendent of Charts. He required all Navy vessels to document daily their position, water temperature, and direction of the current. He compiled this information and found paths in the sea. Would you have read this verse and assumed it was literal? Why / Why not?

_____

_____

Is the Bible literal or mythical stories? Are the events of the Bible historical facts? Explain:

_____

_____

_____

_____

If we must become like children to go to heaven, what does that mean? (Read Matthew 18:3)

_____

_____

_____

_____

_____

_____

What is Jesus saying about the biblical description of earthly things in John 3:12?

Some Christians today do not accept the virgin birth of Jesus. Do you? Explain:

Do you believe the Red Sea really parted and that Israel crossed on dry ground? Explain.

Do you believe in a six-day creation? Why / Why not?

Is it to Satan's advantage to get you to begin doubting God in Genesis 1? Explain.

_____

_____

_____

_____

_____

The Best Commentary on Genesis 1: Scripture

What are the two periods of time Jesus compares in Exodus 20:8-11?

_____

_____

_____

_____

_____

Exodus 20 is the giving of the Ten Commandments. Nine of them are stated in matter-of-fact fashion. One commandment tells says why it is commanded. God said to remember the Sabbath because he wanted them to rest after six days of work just as did.

How long did God want them to work before resting?

☐ 6 Days   ☐ 6 Thousand Years   ☐ 6 Billion Years   ☐ Unknown

Read Exodus 31:16-17.

How long does God say it took him to create everything?

☐ 6 Days   ☐ 6 Thousand Years   ☐ 6 Billion Years   ☐ Unknown

Hebrew Writing Style Reveals Genesis 1 Is Factual

Is Genesis 1 factual or fictional?   ☐ Fact   ☐ Fiction

If Genesis 1 is fiction, what does that do to your faith? Explain:

_____

_____

_____

_____

_____

Answers Magazine, Volume 4 Issue 1, Dr. C. Taylor, Hebrew linguistic expert, points out that Genesis 1 is written in the factual style of Hebrew. There are two distinct styles of Hebrew, poetic and factual. The modifier is placed in one position for poetic writing, and another in factual. Genesis is written in the factual style.

Do experts in Hebrew think Genesis 1 is factual or fictional?   ☐ Fact   ☐ Fiction

Jesus Gives His Opinion About the Creation Week

How long was creation week in Genesis 1? Explain:

_____

_____

_____

_____

How close to the beginning was Abel's murder by Cain? (Jesus's opinion is in Luke 11:49-51)

_____

_____

_____

How long after the beginning until Adam and Eve came along? (Jesus's opinion is in Mark 10:6)

_____
_____
_____
_____
_____
_____

Which Came First, Chicken, or Egg?

How do we know the whether the chicken or the egg came first?

_____

Read Genesis 2:19. Who named the chicken?

_____

The Bible says the chicken was first. God made chickens and Adam named them.

According to the Bible, who named the dinosaurs?

_____
_____

Did trees in the Garden of Eden have rings that indicated age? Why / Why Not? Explain:

_____
_____
_____
_____

The Fossil Record

What does the fossil record really prove about the animal life?

_____

_____

_____

_____

_____

How old do scientists say earth is?

_____

How old did scientists say earth was fifty years ago?

_____

How old did scientists say earth was 100 years ago?

_____

How do we know for sure that the scientific tests are 100 percent accurate?

_____

_____

_____

_____

Does it take faith to believe the scientists are 100 percent accurate? Explain:

_____

_____

_____

Do you think true and accurate science disproves the Bible? Explain:

_____
_____
_____
_____
_____
_____

If science and Scripture appear to contradict, which do you choose to believe? Why?

_____
_____
_____
_____
_____

Some scientists says the fossil record (piles of dead things) occurred billions of years before mankind appeared. Read Romans 5:12. What does the Bible say about this? Explain:

_____
_____
_____
_____
_____
_____
_____

The First Man, and The Mother Of All People

Read 1 Corinthians 15:45. Is it possible Adam was the first man?

_____

Read Genesis 3:20. Is it possible that Eve is the mother of everyone except Adam?

_____

Read Genesis 1:26-31. What day of the creation week was Adam created?

_____

Read Genesis 5:5. How old was Adam when he died?

_____

Since Adam was created on day six and died at the age of 930, is it possible that the creation days are simply "normal" days? Explain what you think and how you came to your opinion on this:

_____

_____

_____

_____

_____

Science versus Scripture on the Subject of Death

What does Science teach about death? Choose one:

☐ Death is a permanent part of history.
☐ Death is a temporary enemy that will be removed.

Read 1 Corinthians 15:26. What does Scripture teach about death? Choose one:

☐ Death is a permanent part of history.
☐ Death is a temporary enemy that will be removed.

Mount Rushmore and Airplanes

Could someone look at the faces on Mount Rushmore and see them possibly as a result of wind and rain erosion? If not, why not? Explain:

_____
_____
_____
_____
_____
_____

Big Bang and Patterns in the Universe

Big Bang multiple choice—check all that apply:

- ☐ Is an attempt by some scientists to explain life without God.
- ☐ Is a big explosion, and explosions always bring order.
- ☐ Obviously explains the beginning of all life.
- ☐ Might have happened, but doesn't explain anything about life.
- ☐ Is one possible way God created everything
- ☐ Is a big explosion, but since explosions cause all particles to spin the same direction—and some planet and moons spin the opposite of their orbits—cannot explain anything.
- ☐ Is a myth, invented by those opposed to serving an intelligent designer.

The smallest objects—protons, neutrons, and electrons—and the largest ones—solar systems—all follow the same pattern. Design confirms a designer. Agree? Why / Why Not? Explain:

_____
_____
_____
_____
_____
_____

A Faith Issue

I now understand it takes faith to believe in Big Bang. ☐ Agree ☐ Disagree

I now understand it takes faith to believe the Bible. ☐ Agree ☐ Disagree

Read Psalm 119:130. How smart or educated must you be to understand the Bible?

_____

Read Proverbs 30:5-6. Does this confirm God's Word as the revelation of truth, or offer the possibility of other interpretations of Genesis 1 and the creation story? Explain:

_____

_____

_____

_____

Read Revelation 22:18-19. What happens to those to twist the Bible to fit their scientific beliefs?

_____

_____

_____

_____

Unless the *context* calls for a symbolic interpretation, it is probably wise to consider that Scripture literal and accurate.

Read Matthew 5:17-18. What did Jesus come to earth to do (in reference to the law)? Explain:

_____

_____

_____

_____

It says "heaven and earth" will "disappear." Will they both really disappear? Even heaven? If so, where will we go when we die? Explain:

_____

_____

_____

_____

A Thousand Years Is Like a Day to God

Read 2 Peter 3:8-10. Check all the statements below that apply to this verse:

☐ Although the context is judgment, it explains creation days.
☐ This proves that the days in Genesis 1 are long time periods.
☐ Although this verse was written in Greek, and Genesis is in Hebrew, it confirms that the Genesis 1 days are actually 1,000 years each.
☐ It's inappropriate to use a Greek word in the New Testament to change the meaning of a Hebrew word in the Old Testament.
☐ This verse is explaining that time is irrelevant to God.

Yom, Hebrew Word for Day

The Hebrew word for *day* is *yom* and is used over twenty thousand times in the Old Testament. It can mean a twenty-four-hour period, the daylight hours, or an extended period of time. However, the only time its meaning in context is questioned is in Genesis 1. Why do you think that is? Who benefits from casting doubt on this? Explain your answer and thoughts behind it:

_____

_____

_____

_____

Summary

I hope the ideas presented here convince you that you can know God means what he says from Genesis 1 to Revelation 22.

Review

Read pages 53-55 in book

What Might Be: A Tangible Heaven

Discussion Questions

1. Will we be able to experience "instant travel" in heaven?
2. Did Jesus do that in His resurrected body? Will our new body be like his?
3. Why call heaven the "real world"? Is it because it's more permanent?
4. How many dimensions are we accustomed to in our world?
5. How many dimensions have scientists discovered?
6. Will we really be able to view events from the past in heaven?
7. Will we have our earthly memories in heaven?
8. There won't be any crying in heaven, will there?

Chapter 2: Prophecy Indications

"Jesus said, 'You're way off base, and here's why: One, you don't know your Bibles; two, you don't know how God works'" (Mark 12:24, MSG). What does Jesus imply about knowing the Scriptures?

_____
_____
_____
_____
_____
_____

Beginning Prayer

Lord, I pray this study of prophecy will be a blessing to all who work through it. I pray people will use these insights to reach lost souls for Your kingdom. I pray that a better understanding of prophecy will open our eyes, ears, minds, and hearts to a deeper understanding of and excitement for heaven. In Jesus's name, Amen.

The Beginnings of Evangelism

Acts records the missionary journeys of Paul. When he got to a new town, he always went first to the Jewish synagogue. Why? Explain:

_____
_____
_____
_____
_____
_____

Read Romans 1:16-17. Who was the gospel to always be offered to first?

_____

If Paul had begun with a non-Jewish audience, how do you think his message would have been received? Why? Explain:

How did Jews respond to that same message? Explain:

By beginning with a Jewish audience there was common ground. What was it?

Did the Jews know what to expect in a Messiah? If so, how? Explain:

___

How did this help the church grow during the early years with an antagonistic government?

___

What I Hope You'll See

God made sure the first coming prophecies were all fulfilled literally. This reveals God's "patterns," and speaks volumes about the second coming ones. But remember, this is not a salvation issue, and you decide for yourself.

Do you think it's possible that God intended for us to see the second coming prophecies as being just as literal as all the first coming ones were? Explain your answer:

___

Prophecy Patterns in the Gospels

In the gospels it often says, "This happened to fulfill prophecy," and it usually quotes the Old Testament prophecy. If this hadn't been pointed out, we seldom would have made the connection. Examples: Read Matthew 1:22, Matthew 2:23, and Matthew 4:14. As we begin this study, would you think that most of the prophecies about the first coming of Christ are symbolic, or literal? Explain your thoughts on this:

Prophecies About the First Coming of Jesus

What are the two categories of Messianic prophecies? What two events do they cover?

Read Isaiah 7:14. What detail about the Messiah does this point to?

Read Micah 5:2. Where does this teach that the Messiah will be born?

Read Numbers 24:17. Who is the "star" that will rise from Jacob? Does this also point to a "star" in the heavens? Explain:

Read Psalm 72:9-10. Did this really happen? What were the gifts?

_____

_____

_____

_____

_____

Read Jeremiah 31:15. What historical event concerning babies does this refer to?

_____

Read Hosea 11:1. Did God actually call Jesus out of Egypt? Explain:

_____

Read Isaiah 40:3. Who was the voice calling in the desert to prepare for Jesus?

_____

Read Isaiah 9:1. Galilee was to be filled with glory? Was it? How?

_____

Read Isaiah 35:5. Was this fulfilled in the life of Jesus? If so, once, or many times?

_____

Read Matthew 17:22. Messiah was to be betrayed by a friend. Was He? If so, by who?

_____

Read Zechariah 11:13 and Matthew 27:3. Were the thirty pieces of silver literally fulfilled? How?

_____

Read Isaiah 53:7 and Matthew 12:15-21. Messiah was foretold not to fight back. Did Jesus? Explain:

_____

Read Isaiah 50:6 and Matthew 26:67. Messiah was foretold to be mocked and spat on. Was Jesus?

_____

Read Isaiah 53:5 and Matthew 27:26. Messiah was foretold to be wounded for our sins. Was Jesus? How?

_____

Read Matthew 12:39. Jesus said the Jews would only get one sign, the sign of Jonah. What was this sign? Did Jesus fulfill it? Explain:

_____

_____

_____

_____

_____

Read Ezekiel 20:49. This is one of many references predicting that Messiah would teach in parables. Now read Matthew 13:36. Did this happen in the life of Jesus?

_____

Read Psalm 118:22 and Mark 8:31. Messiah was to be rejected. Was Jesus rejected?

_____

Read Mark 8:31-32. Jesus predicted a death and resurrection. Who was He talking about?

_____

Read Matthew 27:50. Did Jesus fulfill His own prediction?

_____

Read Psalm 22:16 and Matthew 27:35. Messiah was to have His hands and feed pierced. Did this happen to Jesus?

_____

Read Psalm 22:17 and John 19:36. Messiah was not to have any broken bones. Did Jesus?

Read Psalm 22:18 and Mark 15:24. It was predicted that the Messiah's clothing was to be gambled for. Did this happen with Jesus?

Read Isaiah 53:9 and Matthew 27:60. Messiah was to be buried in a rich man's tomb. Was Jesus?

Read Psalm 16:10 and Matthew 26:52. Messiah was to rise from the dead. Did Jesus?

What Does This Pattern Teach?

Read Mark 12:24. Why does Jesus chastise the Pharisees?

The people in Jesus's day didn't have the entire Bible at their disposal, but we do. Could it be that we will be held responsible for not recognizing God's patterns? Since 100 percent of the first coming prophecies were completely literal, does this teach us anything about the second coming ones? Explain your thoughts on this:

Christians Say the Prophecies Prove Jesus is Messiah

Read Revelation 19:10. What is the purpose of prophecy?

Read Isaiah 9:6. What are the names for Jesus in this verse?

Where will Jesus rule as Messiah?

How long will Jesus rule there?

What assurance do we have that this will happen? Can this be counted on? Explain:

What would an Orthodox Jew point out about Isaiah 9:6? Why don't they see Jesus as Messiah?

How should Christians respond to these objections? True prophets had to be one hundred percent accurate, or they were to be stoned to death. Does Jesus's first coming complete all of these predictions? If not, why not? Explain:

Read Acts 2:29-35. Where is David's throne? Why is this relevant?

Key Verses

Read Luke 24:35-39. After his resurrection, did Jesus have a ghost-like body? Explain:

_____

_____

_____

_____

_____

Read Luke 24:40-43. Was Jesus's resurrection body real and tangible? Did it bear the marks of the cross? Explain:

_____

_____

_____

_____

_____

Read Luke 24:44. What does Jesus imply about the prophecies about him from the prophets and the Psalms? Does He indicate they are just symbols, or that they are real and literal? Explain:

_____

_____

_____

_____

_____

Would you agree that Jesus Christ was the literal fulfillment of all the first coming prophecies about the Messiah, and might also literally fulfill all the second coming ones? Why or why not? Explain:

_____

_____

_____

_____

_____

_____

What Did Jesus Do to the Apostles?

Read Luke 24:45. What did Jesus do to the apostles? Explain:

_____

_____

_____

_____

_____

What Scriptures did Jesus supernaturally enable the apostles to understand?

_____

_____

_____

_____

_____

The NLT says that he opened their minds to understand the Scriptures. The Message states, "He went on to open their understanding of the Word of God, showing them how to read their Bibles this way." The NKJ says he opened their comprehension of the Scriptures. The Complete Jewish Bible says Jesus opened their minds to understand the Old Testament. Young's Literal Translation says he enabled them to understand the "writings." The Bible in Basic English states that he made the writings clear to their minds. The Amplified adds the word "thoroughly." He is telling them that the truth about his comings was in the ancient prophetic writings all along.

Before this event, the disciples asked many questions of Jesus that showed they didn't understand what God's plan was. They argued over who was the greatest, often asked privately what parables meant, wanted children to leave Jesus alone, and suggested he send the crowds away. Once Jesus had opened up their minds to understand the Old Testament prophecies were all literally fulfilled in the life of Jesus of Nazareth, is it reasonable to deduce that they now understood the mystery of God's plan that had previously been so confusing to them? And is it also reasonable to deduce that they will no longer ask irrelevant questions? Explain:

_____
_____
_____
_____
_____

Having Eyes to See and Ears to Hear

Read Deuteronomy 29:2-4. What enables people to understand how God works in this world:

☐ Extensive dedication to Bible study.
☐ Being a witness to a spectacular miracle.
☐ Having a wise teacher point it out for you.
☐ God supernaturally enabling someone to understand.

Read Proverbs 20:12. Who does this Proverb say gives "Ears to hear and eyes to see"?

_____

How do we go about being able to recognize God's activity around us in this world?

_____

Read Amos 3:7. What does this teach?

_____
_____
_____
_____
_____

After Forty Days Discussing Heaven, They Just Had One Question

If you could ask Jesus just one question, what would it be?

_____
_____
_____
_____
_____

Jesus knew He would soon leave the earth, so this was His last chance to cover the most important issues before His departure.

Read Acts 1:3. For forty days after His resurrection, Jesus appeared to the disciples and talked to them about one subject. What was that subject?

_____

Read Acts 1:6. After hearing Jesus lecture for forty days about heaven (the kingdom of God), the disciples asked only one question. What was that question? Was it relevant? Explain:

_____
_____
_____
_____
_____

Read Acts 1:7. What was Jesus's answer to this question about Israel being restored? Choose all the appropriate responses below:

☐ Jesus responded as if that were a dumb question.
☐ Jesus responded as if that were a relevant question.
☐ Jesus's answer focused on the timing, confirming it as true.
☐ Jesus had the perfect opportunity to dispel the notion and possibility of Israel's restoration and He did not, and this greatly disappoints me.

Matthew 24: Past or Future?

Read Matthew 24:15-21. This predicts a time in Israel's future never to be equaled in its reach or intensity for the Jewish people. Does the Roman destruction of Jerusalem in A.D. 70 meet this criteria? If so, how was it worse than the Holocaust? Explain:

_____
_____
_____
_____
_____

Read Matthew 24:22. What detail does this verse add in describing the severity of this?

_____
_____
_____
_____

Read Luke 24:29-31. Immediately after this catastrophic event, what was to happen to the sun, moon, and stars?

_____
_____
_____
_____

Many fail to realize that prophecies often have a double fulfillment: a "near" fulfillment and a "far" fulfillment. Parts of the prophecy point to A. D. 70 in Jerusalem, but other details make this impossible. The Holy Place was desecrated when Rome conquered Jerusalem, Christian Jews did flee the area into the hills, and it was a time of great horror. But we do not see the complete fulfillment. Not even close.

Would you consider the possibility that some Scriptures have a double fulfillment; that some phrases might be fulfilled in one time period while other phrases speak to a different period all together? Explain your thoughts on this:

___

Review

Read pages 73-89 in book

What Might Be: Being in Covenant with God

Discussion Questions

1. Will we really get "training" in heaven?
2. Won't we already know everything when we get to heaven?
3. Will we really study Scripture in eternity?
4. What would be the purpose of studying Scripture in eternity?
5. Why does he use the term "image-bearer" for mankind?
6. Whose image do we bear?
7. How do we bear that image?
8. What similarities are there between us and God?
9. Doesn't other animal life also bear God's image too?
10. Is a study of prophecy relevant for today? If so, how?
11. Is it a shock to learn how much of the Bible concerns prophecy?
12. How does prophecy validate God and Jesus?

13. What is a covenant?

14. How many major covenants are there in the Bible?

15. What does it mean to be in covenant with God?

16. Has God always worked by covenant?

17. What was the first step in the ancient covenant?

18. What did they exchange in the first step? What did the exchange symbolize?

19. How do "put on Christ" in the Christian covenant?

20. What was the second step in the ancient covenant?

21. What did the second step symbolize?

22. Do we have access to God's strength in the new covenant?

23. What was the third step in the ancient covenant?

24. What did the third step symbolize?

25. Who was God's enemy who became man's enemy?

26. Is mankind's true enemy visible or invisible?

27. What was mankind's old enemy that Jesus came to conquer?

28. What was the fourth step in the ancient covenant?

29. What was the purpose of animal sacrifices?

30. What sacrifice did God ask Abraham to make?

31. What sacrifice was God willing to make for mankind?

32. What was the fifth step in the ancient covenant?

33. What is the walk of death under the new covenant?

34. Did it void the covenant if one refused to participate in the walk of death?

35. What was the sixth step in the ancient covenant?

36. Where was the mark on the body usually placed?

37. What was the old covenant mark on the body?

38. What is the new covenant mark on the body (Colossians 2:11-12)?

39. What was the seventh step in the ancient covenant?

40. Under the old covenant, what blessings were available for God's covenant partners?

41. Under the old covenant, what curses were on all covenant breakers?

42. Under the new covenant, what blessings are available for God's covenant partners?

43. Under the new covenant, what curses are on all covenant breakers?

44. What was the eighth step in the ancient covenant?

45. What was the covenant meal called under the old covenant?

46. What is the covenant meal called under the new covenant?

47. What was the ninth step in the ancient covenant?

48. What did Abram change his name to?

49. What is God called in the Bible after the covenant with Abram?

50. What new covenant name do people get today?

51. What was the tenth (the last) step in the ancient covenant?

52. What was the name of Abraham's firstborn son that God asked for?

53. Who did God send to fulfill His part of the covenant?

54. Why did Jesus call Himself, "Son of Man" instead of "Son of God," as He actually was?

Additional questions to consider:

1. What is the first step in your resurrection (Romans 6:3-5)?

2. Is baptism relevant without faith?

3. Is faith relevant without baptism?

4. Is baptism a prophetic act? How?

5. Is it disobedient to reject, ignore, delay, or leave out baptism altogether?

6. What is the true purpose of baptism?

Chapter 3: Satan's Strategy

"This is no afternoon athletic contest that we'll walk away from and forget about in a couple of hours. This is for keeps, a life-or-death fight to the finish against the Devil and all his angels" (Ephesians 6:12, MSG).

Satan Wants to Distort Our View of Heaven

This earth is deteriorating. Erosion, decay, and rust are all symptoms of God's curse.

Select all correct answers below concerning the curse God put on earth:

- ☐ God's curse on earth resulted from mankind's sin.
- ☐ God's curse on earth resulted in painful childbirth.
- ☐ God's curse on earth resulted in having to work for food.
- ☐ God's curse on earth resulted in thorns and stickers.
- ☐ God's curse on earth resulted in expulsion from Eden.
- ☐ God's curse on earth resulted in separation from God.
- ☐ God's curse on earth resulted in separation from Eden.
- ☐ All of the above.

New earth will be forever free of death, disease, and pain, but only faithful covenant people will see it.

Read Romans 8:20. What all was affected when God cursed the earth?

_____

_____

_____

_____

_____

Read Romans 8:21. What will join the saved in freedom from the curse one day?

_____

_____

_____

_____

_____

Read Hebrews 11:1. What is faith?

Do you have faith that the curse on creation will be removed? Explain:

Satan led mankind to sin in Eden, death reigns, and the planet suffers. What all suffers from this?

Read Acts 3:21. What did God promise the prophets long ago?

Do you believe creation will really be restored? If not, why not? Explain:

___

Satan Works to Confuse

Read 2 Corinthians 4:3-4. What has Satan done to the minds of men? Explain:

___

Select all statements below that could apply to Satan's strategy against heaven:

- ☐ Satan makes you think you're not good enough to go to heaven.
- ☐ Satan makes you think heaven will be dull and boring.
- ☐ Satan makes you think heaven will be worship twenty-four-seven.
- ☐ Satan makes you think heaven will be bodiless.
- ☐ Satan makes you think heaven will be eternal harp playing.
- ☐ Satan makes you think you will be a ghost in heaven.
- ☐ Satan makes you think a very lonely place since all of your friends will be in hell.
- ☐ All of the above.

It's a Spiritual Battle for the Mind

Read Luke 8:12. What does Satan steal from people? Explain:

_____
_____
_____
_____
_____
_____
_____

Read Luke 9:43-46. Was it Satan who kept the disciples from understanding? Explain:

_____
_____
_____
_____
_____
_____
_____

Read John 8:31-32. What does knowing truth do for you? Explain:

_____
_____
_____
_____
_____
_____
_____

Read Romans 7:21-23. Did Paul struggle with Satan's power working against him? Explain:

_____

_____

_____

_____

_____

_____

Read 1 Corinthians 2:9. Some say studying heaven is pointless because this passage teaches that we cannot possibly understand it or conceive it. Do you agree? Explain:

_____

_____

_____

_____

_____

_____

Read 1 Corinthians 2:10-12. Select the statements below that are correct based on this passage:

☐ We *can* understand many things about heaven.
☐ The Holy Spirit is involved in revealing heaven to us.
☐ Christians have God's Spirit and can know much about heaven.

Read Ephesians 6:10-18. Rate each statement below as true or false:

☐ T	☐ F	Satan has many strategies to destroy you.
☐ T	☐ F	Your *true* enemies are unseen.
☐ T	☐ F	There are many rulers and authorities in the unseen.
☐ T	☐ F	Satan is not really all that powerful.
☐ T	☐ F	Satan works totally alone.
☐ T	☐ F	Satan wants you to forget to put on God's armor.
☐ T	☐ F	There is no defending against Satan's fiery arrows.
☐ T	☐ F	Praying to God is ineffective against Satan.

Read Revelation 13:6. What is at the core of Satan's strategy against heaven? Explain:

___

Satan Wants Fear to Dominate Our Thoughts

Worry is focusing on what you don't want to happen. Faith and fear cannot coexist. One cancels out the other. Fear is really faith in Satan. Faith in God is a rejection of the fear and worry that Satan wants you to focus on.

Satan has worked to stifle our imagination and creativity about heaven. Be encouraged to think and meditate on heaven.

Read Hebrews 13:14. What does this tell us to look forward to?

___

Read Ephesians 1:18. What does Paul pray for us to understand?

___

Read Philippians 3:19-21. What are we instructed to look forward to? Why? Explain:

___

Do You Trust God Totally?

If your religious background taught something that conflicts with Scripture, which do you do?

☐ Go with the position that's comfortable from my background.
☐ Change my position to match what the Bible says.

Do you think that casting doubt on Genesis 1 leads people to doubt other important things in the Bible, like heaven, the resurrection, and the virgin birth? Explain your thoughts:

___

Read John 16:12-13. We already established that Christians have the Holy Spirit, and that the Holy Spirit reveals things about the future. Could this even include things about heaven? How?

___

Satan's Deception About Heaven

Read John 14:1. Many say there are many ways to heaven. What does this verse say about that?

_____

_____

_____

_____

_____

_____

Read 1 John 4:5-6. What are evil spirits at work doing throughout the world? Explain:

_____

_____

_____

_____

_____

_____

Read 2 Timothy 4:3-4. At some point, most people won't be interested in the truth of God. Are we at that point today? Explain and discuss:

_____

_____

_____

_____

_____

_____

Satan Uses Misdirection, Deception, and Scriptural Misapplication

Greek was the perfect language for the original text of the Bible because it is so descriptive. In English, for example, we "love" pizza, an adventure, or our spouse. The first applies to taste, the second to excitement, and the third to relationship. But in the Greek, these realities are communicated by three completely different words.

Similarly, some Bible passages seem to discredit the idea of a tangible eternal kingdom and must be dealt with individually, looking at the original Greek, the context, and other passages that seem to contradict this.

Read 2 Timothy 3:16. What does this teach? Explain. Can Scripture contradict itself?

_____

_____

_____

_____

_____

_____

Jesus Said His Kingdom Was Not of This World

"Jesus said, 'My kingdom is not of this world. If it were, my servants would fight to prevent my arrest by the Jews. But now my kingdom is from another place.'" John 18:36. What is Jesus saying about His kingdom? Explain:

_____

_____

_____

_____

_____

_____

The *Bible Knowledge Commentary* says the kingdom, "Comes not by rebellion but by submission to God." *Wiersbe's Expository Outlines* says, "When He returns, He will establish His kingdom on earth." And the Jamieson, Fausset, and Brown Commentary states, "He does not say it is not 'in' or 'over,' but it is not 'of this world,' that is, in its origin and nature."

But Jesus Said the Earth Would Disappear

Read Matthew 24:35. What does this say will happen to God's Word?

_____

_____

_____

_____

_____

_____

_____

This also seems to say that heaven and earth will both completely disappear. If that is so, where will we spend eternity? Hell? Explain:

_____

_____

_____

_____

_____

_____

At first glance this appears to contradict other verses that indicate a "heaven on earth" possibility. The Greek word here for *earth* is literally "the soil," and the Greek here for *heaven* means "the abode of God." Obviously, God's "abode" will never disappear.

The answer may lie in understanding that God "destroyed" earth with a flood, but it is still here. In 2 Peter 3:7, God reveals his plan to destroy by fire. Therefore, the likely answer that best fits is that just as the waters of the flood purified earth long ago, a fire will purify it in the future.

Read 1 Corinthians 3:12-15. What will burn in God's fire one day? What will remain? Explain:

_____

_____

_____

_____

Jesus Said Some of the Disciples Would See the Kingdom Come

Read Matthew 16:28. Jesus is stating a fact about the future to His disciples. What is it?

_____

Since all these disciples lived to see the day of Pentecost, why didn't Jesus say they would all see the kingdom come? John was in the audience when Jesus made this statement. What did he see in a vision on the island of Patmos that might qualify as "seeing" the coming of the kingdom of God? Explain:

_____

_____

_____

_____

_____

_____

The Greek here means "a person, a body, or a man." So although Pentecost did usher in the beginning of the church—the first phase of the kingdom—Jesus must be talking about something else; probably the actual beginning of eternity: the second coming.

Daniel 10, Interface Between Seen and Unseen

Read Daniel 10:2 and 12-13. How long had Daniel been praying?

_____

What kept this angel from getting there sooner?

_____

Who came to help with the battle?

_____

Where was the first spirit prince from that this angel had been fighting?

_____

Read Daniel 10:20-21. Who did this angel expect to fight after the spirit prince of Persia?

_____

In history, what world power conquered the Medo-Persian Empire?

_____

When Daniel began to pray, what began to happen in the unseen? Explain:

_____

_____

_____

_____

_____

Some say God offers three possible answers to prayer:
 1) Yes.
 2) No.
 3) Maybe later.

Do you agree with this statement as a fourth possibility in regard to prayer?
 "God's answer is on its way, but is being delayed by evil forces." ☐ Agree   ☐ Disagree

Read Ephesians 6:12. Is prayer human intervention into invisible battles? If so, how? Explain:

_____

_____

_____

_____

_____

"Enemies" is plural. Do we have more than one evil, unseen enemy?

_____

Many Demons Are Named in Scripture

Read 2 Kings 17:29-31. In the blanks below, list every demon listed in this passage:

_____

_____

_____

_____

_____

_____

_____

In the same order, list the city, region, or nation each of these demons were ruling over:

_____

_____

_____

_____

_____

_____

_____

Read Psalm 106:36-38. When they sacrificed their children to idols, who accepted? Explain:

_____

_____

_____

_____

Read 1 Corinthians 10:20. Sacrifices offered to idols were actually being offered to whom?

Read 1 Peter 5:8. What is Satan's primary activity? Explain:

Jesus Confirms Satan's Kingdom

Read Matthew 4:8-10. What did Satan offer Jesus?

Jesus didn't dispute Satan's claim on all the kingdoms of the world. Why? Explain:

Select each statement below that is true:

- ☐ Jesus was in charge of the kingdoms of the world but didn't want to say it at the time.
- ☐ Adam's sin in Eden caused him to relinquish authority to Satan, so the kingdoms of the world really were Satan's.
- ☐ Jesus was silent on the subject of Satan's authority over all the kingdoms of the world because Satan actually *was* in control.
- ☐ Jesus meant to say, "You have nothing to offer me because these are already mine," but forgot to.

Read 2 Corinthians 4:4. What is Satan called in this passage? Why? Explain:

_____
_____
_____
_____
_____
_____

But Didn't Jesus Say He Had All Authority?

Read Matthew 28:18. Who has all authority? What is included in that authority? Explain:

_____
_____
_____
_____
_____
_____

Read Ephesians 2:2. Who is being discussed as the "ruler of the kingdom of the air"? Why?

_____

Read Hebrews 2:8. Has Jesus exercised His authority over all things? When?

_____

_____

_____

_____

_____

_____

The Final Blow to Satan's Authority

Read 1 Corinthians 15:24-26. In the end, who will the kingdom be turned over to?

_____

Who is in the kingdom now that will be destroyed at that time?

_____

How long will Christ reign there?

_____

Who is the last enemy there He will destroy?

_____

Two Phases of the Kingdom

Read Matthew 12:28. What characterizes the coming of the kingdom?

_____

Read Acts 10:38. What did Jesus do for those who were under the power of Satan?

_____

According to Jesus and the example of His ministry, the removal of demons, sickness, and evil spirits of every kind characterize the kingdom's coming.

The church was chosen to usher in phase one of the kingdom. Read Matthew 16:15-18.

How did Peter know who Jesus was?

_____

Does it sound like the power of hell will be attacking God's church? Explain:

_____

Who will win the battle between the power of hell and heaven? Why?

_____

Read Revelation 21:3-4. Where does God plan to live for eternity?

_____

Will there be tears there? If not, what will God wipe away? Explain:

_____

What will happen to death, sickness, and pain?

_____

Summary

Satan's strategy against God: distorting the truth about heaven in every possible way.

Review

Read pages 112-114 in book

What Might Be: The True Location of the Kingdom

Discussion Questions

1. Why does the angel call the New Testament the New Covenant?
2. Read Matthew 13:36-43.
3. Who is the "Son of Man"?

4. What is "the field" in the story?

5. What do the "good seeds" represent in the story?

6. What do the "weeds" in the story represent?

7. Who planted the "weeds"?

8. What does the "harvest" represent?

9. What happens to the "weeds" in the end?

10. What do the angels do in the end?

11. Where do the angels put the "weeds" in the end?

12. If the angels remove the "weeds," what group is left in the kingdom?

13. Was Jesus's resurrection body tangible or ghostlike?

14. Could Jesus eat and drink real food in His resurrection body?

15. Will there be eating and drinking in heaven?

16. How many dimensions are there in our present world?

17. Could God have created more dimensions that we are currently aware of?

18. What is the maximum number of dimensions God could create?

19. Read Genesis 28:12-13. In Jacob's dream, what connected heaven and earth?

20. Could God and angels really be that close, just beyond our ability to see them?

21. Could the heavenly realm be tangible yet unseen?

22. Could the seen and unseen truly be combined one day?

23. Would you agree with this definition of heaven: "Wherever God is"?

24. If that is feasible, could it be that the original, perfect earth was part of heaven? Discuss.

Chapter 4: Purification by Fire

"They conveniently forget that long ago all the galaxies and this very planet were brought into existence out of watery chaos by God's word. Then God's word brought the chaos back in a flood that destroyed the world. The current galaxies and earth are fuel for the final fire. God is poised, ready to speak his word again, ready to give the signal for the judgment and destruction of the desecrating skeptics" (2 Peter 3:5-7, MSG).

"I heard the count and saw both horses and riders in my vision: fiery breastplates on the riders, lion heads on the horses breathing out fire and smoke and brimstone. With these three weapons—fire and smoke and brimstone—they killed a third of the human race" (Revelation 9:16-18, MSG).

Fear the Fire of the Coming Wrath of God

I went through my Bible searching for heaven, and some unexpected patterns emerged. One of these was the idea that purification fires from God will purge the planet of all evil and evil people. They seemed connected with judgment, punishment, and God's wrath. It's easy to associate fire with hell. The connection I suggest here is subtle.

Read 1 Peter 1:7. What is the symbolic fire in this reference used for?

_____

Read 1 Corinthians 3:13-15. Fire is a big part of judgment day. What does it do? Explain:

_____

_____

_____

_____

How can someone lose an eternal reward they have yet to receive? Explain:

_____

_____

_____

_____

MY SEARCH FOR THE REAL HEAVEN Workbook

Does the idea of rewards from God motivate you to be more active in your faith? Explain:

_____

_____

_____

_____

_____

Read 1 Chronicles 28:9. Describe the level of detail God knows about you.

_____

_____

_____

_____

Read Proverbs 20:27. Describe the level of detail God knows about you.

_____

_____

_____

_____

Read Luke 5:22. Describe the level of detail God knows about you.

_____

_____

_____

_____

Read Acts 1:24. Describe the level of detail God knows about you.

_____

_____

_____

_____

_____

_____

Read Hebrews 4:13. Describe the level of detail God knows about you.

_____

_____

_____

_____

_____

_____

What sort of "account" must we give to God one day? _____

Read Matthew 6:3-4. Describe the level of detail God knows about you.

_____

_____

_____

_____

_____

_____

What will God do for Christians with this intimate knowledge of their deeds?

Remember, salvation is a gift, but rewards are earned. Don't confuse these.

Purification by Fire: Old Testament Support

Read Genesis 3:8. Before sin, what did God and Adam do together (apparently regularly)?

Read Genesis 3:23-24. How was fire involved in Adam and Eve's banishment from Eden?

After sin and banishment from Eden, every time God appears in Scripture, there is fire.

Read Exodus 19:18 and Deuteronomy 33:2. Describe the fiery scene when the Lord descended onto Mount Sinai:

_____

_____

_____

_____

_____

_____

_____

Read 2 Kings 2:11-17. What appeared from the unseen to pick up Elijah?

_____

_____

_____

_____

_____

_____

Read 2 Chronicles 7:1-2. Describe the fiery scene at the dedication of the temple.

_____

_____

_____

_____

_____

_____

Read Psalm 18:9-15. Describe what the lightning and fire do in this passage.

_____

_____

_____

_____

_____

_____

Read Psalm 37:9-11. What will happen to those who have faith in God?

_____

What will happen to the wicked—those who don't have faith in God?

_____

Read Psalm 37:34. What will God give those who patiently wait on Him?

_____

Read Psalm 46:6. What does it sound like when God speaks?

_____

Read Psalm 50:1-3. Where will God stand on judgment day? Describe the scene:

_____

_____

_____

_____

_____

Read Psalm 58:9-11. Who rejoices on judgment day, and who is swept away in fire? Explain:

_____
_____
_____
_____

Read Psalm 68:1-2. What will happen to the wicked in the end?

_____
_____
_____
_____
_____

Read Psalm 97:3. What happens to all of God's enemies in the end?

_____
_____
_____
_____
_____

Read Psalm 97:4-6, and 9. What will lightning and fire do in the end?

_____
_____
_____
_____
_____

What will God be heralded as king of in the end?

Read Psalm 104:35. What will happen to all the sinners on the earth?

At that point, who will be left on the earth?

Read Psalm 119:119. What will happen to all the wicked people on the earth?

At that point, who will be left on the earth?

Read Psalm 144:5. In the end, what will happen to the mountains when God touches them?

Read Proverbs 10:30. In the end, what will happen to the wicked?

At that point, who will be left on the earth?

Read Isaiah 30:27-29. When God arrives in the end, how is fire involved?

What will the godly be doing at this point?

Where do the people go up to then?

_____

Read Isaiah 66:15. How is fire involved at the coming of the Lord?

_____

_____

_____

_____

_____

_____

Read Joel 2:1-3. On the day of the Lord (judgment day), what does the fire do?

_____

_____

_____

_____

_____

Read Micah 1:3-4. What happens to the earth as the Lord comes down onto it?

_____

_____

_____

_____

_____

Fire will remove every ungodly person and thing on earth. Those left after the fire will be kind, humble, and faithful to God. All will live and sleep in peace and safety, and next passages indicate a reversal of Babel, where God confused the languages. There will be only one language and a unified people. This makes sense in light of the removal of the curse caused by rebellion.

Read Zephaniah 3:8-13. What will consume the earth?

___

Where will the people assemble?

___

Who will be there?

___

Will there be food?

___

Will there be any fear?

___

Read Zechariah 13:8-9.

What percent of the people will die in the fire?

___

What will happen to those who pass through the fire and remain?

___

What will they do after they survive the fire?

___

Whose people will the survivors be?

Purification by Fire: New Testament Support

Read Matthew 5:5. What did Jesus say would happen to the earth?

___

Read Matthew 6:10. This is from the famous "Lord's Prayer." Christians were to pray for the kingdom to come.

Didn't the kingdom come at Pentecost? If so, did it come fully, or partially? Explain:

_____

_____

_____

_____

_____

What did Jesus teach in verse 10 that would accompany the coming of the kingdom? Explain:

_____

Some say the church completely fulfills this requirement, but that may not be totally the case. Consider this:

How is God's will done in heaven? Choose the best answer:

☐ Perfectly, completely, and immediately.
☐ Pretty well, partially, and eventually.

When God calls His messenger angels to send word to someone, do they put it on their calendar, or ask God if next week is soon enough? No. In the unseen, God's will is always done perfectly, completely, and immediately. Does the church do this? No. However, when Jesus comes back, will His will be done perfectly, completely, and immediately at that time? Yes.

Chose all statements below that make sense in light of all the passages studied so far:

☐ Although the Lord's Prayer was given by Jesus, knowing it would be thousands of years before His return, it was only really applicable until Pentecost, when the kingdom came.
☐ Jesus wanted us to pray for the kingdom to come to earth.
☐ The meek really will inherit the earth.
☐ All the ungodly will be removed from the earth.
☐ Jesus got mixed up, and this part of the prayer should have been left out.
☐ Jesus got mixed up, and this part of the prayer should now be worded, "Thy kingdom has come."
☐ We can't possibly know this answer even if we want to.
☐ The church is the only fulfillment of this there ever will be.
☐ I am set in my thinking about heaven, and no amount of study or reasoning will change my opinion.
☐ In the final phase of the coming kingdom, the evil people will be sorted out, and only the godly (like the meek) will remain.

Read Matthew 13:24-30 and 36-43.

What does this seem to suggest will happen to the weeds (all the evil people) in the end?

_____

After all the evil people are removed from the kingdom (earth), where are the righteous people?
    Read Matthew 13:47-50. Choose the order the Scripture specifies:
    ☐ Angels separate the wicked from the righteous and throw them out of the kingdom into the fire.
    ☐ Angels come and take the good people somewhere else as the earth burns up.
    ☐ Angels divide earth into two sections, one section for good people and one section for evil people.

Parables are often called "earthly stories with heavenly meanings." What do you see as the heavenly meaning of this important story in regard to where the kingdom is, who gets the kingdom, and who is removed from the kingdom? Explain:

_____

_____

_____

_____

_____

_____

Read Matthew 22:1-13.

What do you think the wedding banquet represents?

_____

Why would someone refuse to come? Who do you think these people are?

_____

What did the king do to the city in his great anger?

_____

What do the wedding clothes represent?

_____

MY SEARCH FOR THE REAL HEAVEN WORKBOOK

What happens to the person not properly dressed for the banquet?

_____

Read Galatians 3:27 and answer these same two questions:

_____

What do the wedding clothes represent?

_____

What happens to the person not properly dressed for the banquet?

_____

Read Matthew 25:31-46.

When Jesus comes, who will be gathered before Him?

_____

What will He do next?

_____

What happens to the "sheep" (good people) on His right?

☐ They stay and enjoy the kingdom where they are.
☐ They are taken away to enjoy the kingdom somewhere else.

Read Mark 9:49. Who must experience God's holy fire on some level?

_____

Read Luke 13:29. What happens after God's holy fire has done its work? Describe:

_____

_____

_____

_____

Read Hebrews 1:2. What did God promise Jesus as an inheritance? Explain in detail:

_____

_____

_____

_____

_____

What is included in the "universe" God promised to Jesus?

_____

_____

_____

_____

The Greek means earth will be fully destroyed, like changing your outer garment. God will declare it obsolete. The mantle (outer layer of earth) will be peeled back and changed.

Read Hebrews 1:10-12.

What is described as the work of God's hands?

☐ Heaven and earth.   ☐ Only heaven.

Select any possible changes from list below:

☐ Earth might return to a pre-flood condition.
☐ Earth might return to a pre-curse condition.
☐ Life spans extended (eternally).
☐ Angels and mankind enjoy life together.
☐ Celebrations and parties.
☐ Feasts and wonderful banquets.
☐ Restored access for mankind to the tree of life.
☐ Eternal access to God and the river of life.
☐ Enjoyment of rewards for every good deed done.
☐ All of the above.

Read 2 Peter 3:3-7.

God once "destroyed" earth by flood. What will "destroy" it next time?

_____

When will that happen (on what day)?

_____

Who will be hurt by this event?

_____

Read 2 Peter 3:11-13.

Should Christians dread the judgment day?

_____

What will be the result of the fire as far as earth is concerned?

_____

Conclusion

Earth was once destroyed by a flood yet still remains. It is destined for destruction by fire yet will remain. The fire will remove all evil and evil people, allowing restoration and resurrection.

Review

Read pages 136-138 in book

What Might Be: Dad Visits Lazarus and the Rich Man

Discussion Questions

1. Will we really be able to visit with Bible characters in heaven?

2. Why does the angel call this earth the "shadowland"? Who else called it that?

3. Why is Jamie called a "newcomer" to heaven? Have some been there a long time? I thought you were just asleep from the time you die until the resurrection. Discuss. (2 Corinthians 5:8.)

4. Could it be that the saved will have multiple angelic servants?

5. Aren't parables just allegories, just symbolic?

6. Will we learn new things in heaven about Bible stories in Scripture (like the rich man's name)?

7. Will there really be water in heaven?

Chapter 5: Resurrection and Our New Body

Read 1 Corinthians 6:14. God's power raised Jesus from the grave. What about us?

___

One Last Handwritten Note from Dad

In an old safe, my brother and I found an envelope from Dad addressed to the two of us:

"To: Steve and Kendal
   This envelope is not to be opened except in Jamie's presence—if he is no longer living and this is still unopened, then destroy without opening—it is not important.
   Dad 1/09/2000"

Consider all the possibilities. What would you do?

___

___

___

___

___

Here's what I did:
   We agonized for several hours. Then my brother held it up and said, "You're the oldest. You decide." Now the burden was all on me. "Well," I began, "There is a resurrection. We are going to have to face Dad again. When we do, I want him to be proud of us. I don't want to have to shuffle up with my head down in shame and say, 'Hi, Dad. Sorry, but we opened that envelope you said not to.' So we burned it.
   Hebrews 11 is a list of many faithful servants. Was your mother, father, grandmother, or grandfather a woman or man of faith? If so, they are part of that list of people who will be honored one day for their faithfulness?
   Now read Hebrews 12:1. Many versions begin with this chapter with the word *therefore*, which ties together the thoughts from these chapters.

Defeating Death

Read 1 Corinthians 15:26. What is the last enemy to be destroyed?

Is the Physical World Evil?

Some say that if it's physical, it's evil. Does this agree with Scripture?

Read Genesis 1:31. What did God say about creation after He finished it?

Satan isn't physical. Is he evil?

Resurrection Is Motivation for Caring for Our Current Physical Body

Read 1 Corinthians 6:13-14. This is God's instructions for sexual purity.
If you are a Christian, who does your body belong to?
Choose all correct statements about the body below:

☐ Christians should care for the body because it is God's.
☐ Christians should care for the body to serve God's purposes.
☐ Christians should care for the body because God will raise it.

The DNA or your current body is part of your eternal DNA, or there is no need to resurrect it.

Physical Resurrection Was a View Shared by Many Bible Figures

Read Hebrews 11:19. Did Abraham believe in a physical resurrection?

What did he think was going to happen with Isaac?

Read Job 19:25-27. Did Job believe in a physical resurrection?

_____

What did Job expect to do?

_____

Read Psalm 16:9-11. Did David believe in a physical resurrection?

_____

What did David expect to happen after his death?

_____

Read Matthew 27:51-53. Choose the correct answer below:

☐ When Jesus resurrected, many godly people died.
☐ When Jesus resurrected, many godly people were also raised.
☐ When Jesus resurrected, many godly people appeared as ghosts.

What would you say to someone after you attended their funeral then saw them walking again?

_____

Resurrection Teachings and Examples in Scripture

Read Romans 6:3-4. How do we become joined to Christ's death?

_____

What act specifically ties you to the resurrection, allowing you to live a new life here?

_____

Read 1 Thessalonians 4:16.

What two things will accompany the arrival of the Lord?

_____

Who will rise from the grave first?

_____

If your physical DNA isn't a permanent part of your eternity, what would be the purpose of rising from our graves? The Greek here for *rise* means "to stand upright again."

Jesus Rose From the Grave

Read Mark 16:9. Read 1 Corinthians 15:20-23. Elijah raised a widow's son from death, and Jesus raised Lazarus after four days in the grave. So why is Jesus called the firstfruits of those who have died? Explain:

_____

_____

_____

_____

_____

_____

The Dead Rich Man Wanted Water

Read Luke 16:19-31.

When the beggar died, what happened to him?

_____

When the rich man died, what happened to him?

_____

Where did the Lazarus man go?

_____

What did the rich man want? How does what we want affect our spiritual lives?

_____

Did the rich man have a body and a tongue in hell?

_____

How far apart were Lazarus and the rich man?

Were they able to get together? How, or why not?

What did the rich man want next?

Did the rich man remember his past life?

What did he remember about his family?

What did the rich man call the place he was in?

Did Abraham send word to the rich man's family? Why/why not? Explain:

Would everyone in the world believe in heaven and hell if someone was resurrected from the dead? Why/why not? Explain:

Scripture Says Our New Body Will Be Like Jesus's Resurrection Body

Read Philippians 3:21. What does God have the power to do with our body?

Whose body will our resurrection body be like? How? Explain:

There Are Bodies in Heaven

Read 1 Corinthians 15:40. Will heaven be experienced in a body or bodiless? Explain:

_____

_____

_____

_____

_____

_____

Resurrection of Earth Is Also Promised

Read Acts 3:20-22. How long will Jesus wait to return for the second coming?

_____

What will He do to the creation when He returns?

_____

Read Romans 8:20-21. What percent of creation was affected by God's curse after sin?

_____

What is the creation currently in "bondage" to? Explain and describe:

_____

_____

_____

_____

_____

Will this bondage last forever, or will it end? If so, how and when? Explain and describe:

_____

_____

_____

_____

_____

_____

Read Revelation 21:5. What does God plan to do with creation?

_____

Is this for certain, or just a possibility (according to Scripture)? Explain:

_____

Even the Sea Will Give Up the Dead

Read Revelation 20:13. What will happen to those who have died at sea? Explain:

_____

If your current DNA isn't part of eternity, there's no need to gather bodies from the sea.

Seeds Are the Metaphor of Choice Describing Our Eternal Bodies

Paul said some would be confused about the resurrection. He said the idea of a literal, physical resurrection would be attacked or dismissed. He even called these people foolish:

Read 1 Corinthians 15:35-43. Select all true statements below that illustrate our eternal bodies.

- ☐ Seeds are used as an illustration of our eternal body.
- ☐ Seeds are placed in the ground, just like our dead body.
- ☐ Seeds come to life again, just like our new, eternal body.
- ☐ A farmer doesn't plant an entire corn plant, just a kernel, just like our new, eternal body.
- ☐ The plant that comes from the seed has everything the seed had plus much more, just like our new, eternal body.
- ☐ Our eternal body will just be a spirit.

- ☐ Just as there are different kinds of earthly flesh (humans, birds, fish, etc), there are different kinds of eternal bodies (God, angels, resurrected humans, etc.).
- ☐ Your current body will be resurrected, then discarded.
- ☐ Your current body will be resurrected, then transformed.

Read 1 Corinthians 15:44. The Greek for *spiritual bodies* means "concretely supernatural." In eternity, we will have a concrete, tangible, supernatural, immortal body. How does this compare to what you have always believed? Explain:

_____

_____

_____

_____

Butterflies Illustrate This Now

Butterflies are probably the best example of the future reality of physical resurrection. An ugly, slimy, dirty caterpillar is buried in a cocoon and emerges as a beautiful, colorful, dainty, ornate flying creature. A worm original DNA is changed, enhanced, and improved.

Springtime Is a Yearly Example

Every spring, when the grass turns from brown to green, we see an example of the resurrection. When the leaves put out new leaves, and their silhouette transforms from outlines of branches and limbs to puffy balls against the blue sky, we see an example of the resurrection. Winter brings death and hibernation, but spring brings restored life and hope. All by God's design?

What other examples in creation can you think of that help illustrate our future resurrection?

_____

_____

_____

_____

Three Physical Bodies Are Currently in Heaven

Read Genesis 5:24. Who is this, and what happened to his body?

_____

Read 2 Kings 2:11. Who is this, and what happened to his body?

_____

Read Luke 24:50-51. Who is this, and what happened to his body?

_____

When Jesus descended, did he shed his skin and bones? Describe this ascension:

_____

_____

_____

_____

_____

Many Christians Are Confused About Resurrection

Although they believe in an afterlife, many Christians don't believe in the resurrection. The definition of *resurrection* is "a dead body coming back to life." Anything less is not a resurrection. Resurrection comes from the Middle English *resurrecioun*. The late Latin word is *resurrectio*, the act of rising from the dead. The root is *resurgere*, to rise from the dead or to rise again.

Do you believe in a physical resurrection or just an eternal, spiritual-only existence? Explain:

_____

_____

_____

_____

Read John 8:43-45. Remember, God invented the languages. When the language God uses on this is unclear, what does this Scripture say the problem is? Explain.

___

Read Acts 17:16-18. What did the people of Athens think of the idea of a resurrection?

___

Resurrection, then transformation, is the scriptural truth that some have ignored or redefined.

Read 1 Corinthians 15:50-54. Select all biblically accurate statements below:

- ☐ Flesh and blood cannot go to heaven; therefore, this body will have nothing to do with eternity.
- ☐ Flesh and blood can't go to heaven, but this body will have something to do with it; although, it's somewhat of a mystery.
- ☐ Flesh and blood cannot go to heaven, but this body will be changed to become eternal.
- ☐ The transformation of our flesh and blood bodies into immortal ones will occur instantaneously.
- ☐ The transformation of our flesh and blood bodies into immortal ones will occur at the last trumpet.
- ☐ The transformation of our flesh and blood bodies into immortal ones will signal the victory of life over death.
- ☐ The DNA of our flesh and blood bodies will be eliminated.
- ☐ The DNA of our flesh and blood bodies will be transformed.

Rising from the Grave

Read 1 Thessalonians 4:15-18.

What will rise from the grave?

___

Will some people be alive when Jesus returns?

___

List the sequence of events at the second coming according to this passage:

Read John 5:25-29. Will dead people be able to hear again one day?

Will everyone be able to hear or just the godly ones?

Will people actually be able to hear God from inside their coffins in the ground?

Will everyone rise from the grave or just the godly people?

Read 2 Corinthians 5:8-9. Once you have left your earthly body, where will you be?

What They Thought When Jesus Died

Read Luke 24:21. What did the disciples think when Jesus died?

What Did Resurrection Mean to the Disciples?

Select all correct answers:

- ☐ If He could rise from death, so can we!
- ☐ Victory is assured!
- ☐ The enemy will be crushed.
- ☐ Jesus is King!

Read Acts 1:1-3. From the resurrection until Pentecost (about forty days), Jesus appeared to the disciples to prove He was actually alive and discussed one topic. What was it?

_____

After forty days of Jesus discussing heaven, what is the one question the disciples had?

_____

Select all correct statements about Jesus's answer to that one question:

- ☐ Jesus said, "There will not be an earthly kingdom."
- ☐ Jesus said, "The timing of that event is a secret."

What Will Our Body Be Like?

Read Philippians 3:20-21. Christians are already citizens of _____.

Describe how Christians should feel about death and about the second coming of Jesus:

_____

_____

_____

_____

_____

When Jesus returns what will He bring under His control?

_____

Jesus will come in power. What does that power have the ability to do?

_____

Describe your thoughts about our eternal body:

_____
_____
_____
_____
_____
_____

Read Luke 24:13-31, the story of Jesus on the road to Emmaus after His resurrection.

Why didn't these men recognize Jesus?

_____

What were they discussing on that road?

_____

What had they hoped about Jesus?

_____

How long had He been dead?

_____

Did they still hope?

_____

They knew Jesus's body was missing. Did they believe He had been raised?

_____

How did Jesus respond to this? What did He call them?

_____

What did Jesus use to prove He actually was the Redeemer they had hoped for? Explain:

_____

_____

_____

_____

_____

Jesus was in His resurrected, transformed body when this event occurred. Did He refuse to eat with them since He was no longer "flesh and blood," or was He able to eat and drink, just as He had before?

_____

_____

_____

_____

_____

What method did Jesus use to leave them when He departed?

_____

Read John 20:19. How did Jesus get to where the disciples were? Explain:

_____

_____

_____

_____

_____

Read John 20:17. When Mary first saw Jesus after His resurrection, He told her not to touch Him or hold on to Him. Why? Explain:

Read Luke 24:39. Why did Jesus offer his hands and side to be touched this time? Explain:

Read 2 Corinthians 5:1-5. What camp item is compared to our current body?

Who will build our eternal home (body)?

Our current body is mortal. Describe our eternal body in comparison:

Read Luke 24:37-43. Did Jesus have skin and bones after the resurrection?

_____

Was Jesus able to eat food and drink water after the resurrection?

_____

Read Romans 8:23. Jesus is the "firstfruits" of resurrection. Who gets "firstfruits" of the Spirit?

_____

Christians are adopted into what family?

_____

This adoption has an eternal effect on our bodies. What is that effect? Explain:

_____

_____

_____

_____

_____

Your body will be like his: tangible but immortal. This is what you have to look forward to.

Review

Read pages 160-165 in book

What Might Be: Seeing What God Sees

Discussion Questions

1. Will we really meet Adam, Enoch, Moses, and Paul in eternity?
2. What will you ask each one when you meet?
3. Will we really "grow" as individuals from our interaction with others in heaven?
4. Will we still pray when we get to heaven?
5. What is prayer? Talking to God? Will we do more, or less of that in eternity?
6. Won't we understand God's love completely when we first arrive in heaven?
7. Will we have experiences in heaven that will enhance our love for Him?
8. Why does the angel call the Bible a "guidebook"?
9. What has Satan "captured" that Jesus came to "retake"? Discuss.
10. What is the final enemy Jesus says He will defeat?
11. What are the two kingdoms as defined in Scripture?
12. What battle is raging in the unseen?
13. How do we win the battle?
14. Is there really a war going on in the unseen that most are unaware of?
15. Who is going to win that war?
16. What book in the Bible reveals many details of that victory?
17. Why does the angel call the unseen world the "real" one?
18. What must be done to "join Jesus in death"?
19. What does it mean to be "buried with Christ"?

Chapter 6: Connecting Eternity, Heaven, and New Earth

Read Isaiah 66:22. How long will the new earth last?

_____

Read Colossians 3:1. Christians are commanded to focus on what?

_____

Where is Jesus Christ right now?

_____

The Bible talks about eternity, heaven, the kingdom, the church, and an eternal new earth. Let's see if we can connect the dots on all this.

Living on a Destroyed Planet

Read 2 Peter 3:5-6. God destroyed earth with a flood. He promised—with a rainbow as the sign—that he would never destroy it with water again. Destruction didn't mean annihilation. It meant purification. Take a moment here and describe what you think the earth was like before the flood, including the water canopy above the sky (Genesis 1:6).

_____

_____

_____

_____

_____

God Plans to Destroy It Again

Read 2 Peter 3:7. What will God use to "destroy" earth next time?

_____

MY SEARCH FOR THE REAL HEAVEN Workbook

What is that day called throughout the Scriptures?
_____

Who will be destroyed in that day of judgment?
_____

Since the flood didn't annihilate earth, is it possible (perhaps even probable) that fire won't annihilate it either?
_____

Read 2 Peter 3:10. How will the day of the Lord come?
_____

What will happen to the earth?
_____

God's Land Plans

Read Proverbs 2:21-22. Who will ultimately remain in the land?
_____

What will happen to the wicked in reference to the land?
_____

Read Psalm 37 and answer the following questions:

What do the first two verses reveal about what God plans for evil people?
_____

What does verse 3 suggest to you about the godly people?
_____

What does verse 9 suggest to you about the godly people?
_____

What does verse 11 suggest to you about the godly people?

_____

What does verse 18 suggest to you about the godly people?

_____

What does verse 22 suggest to you about the godly people?

_____

What does verse 27 suggest to you about the godly people?

_____

What does verse 29 suggest to you about the godly people?

_____

What will happen to those who hope in the Lord (verse 34)?

_____

Read Matthew 5:1-5. What did Jesus teach would happen to the meek and humble?

_____

In the Greek, this is literally a prayer for God to bring his realm of reign to earth.

The Bible only records one prayer of Jesus. God knew it would be recorded and quoted for centuries. Do you think that He gave them this phrase just to apply to the few dozen people who would pray it forty days? It's possible but not probable. However, if there were plans to bring the kingdom to earth, a prayer like this would make sense, wouldn't it?

Five Earths in Scripture

1. Original earth. Read Genesis 1:31. How did God describe the original, physical earth?

_____

Read Genesis 3:8. How did Adam know it was God he heard walking in Eden?

_____

Read Genesis 9:2. What does this reveal about animals on the original earth?

___

Original earth was good and perfect in every possible way. But it came to an end because of the curse invoked by God after sin. This led to the second earth.

2. Cursed earth. Read Genesis 3:17-18. Describe the changes the curse brought.

___

Read Romans 8:20. How much of creation was affected by God's curse?

___

Read Romans 5:12. What was the effect of the curse on humans? What does this Scripture say about death prior to sin and the curse?

___

Read Genesis 3:16. What two affects did the curse have on women? (Hint for second one: woman's desire for something would be given to the man.)

1. ___

2. ___

3. Post-Flood Earth. Read Genesis 7:11. What directions did the water come from? Explain:

___

___

___

___

Read Genesis 9:2. How was wildlife different after the flood?

___

Read Genesis 9:3. What did God now authorize to eat that was eaten previously?

_____

Read Genesis 1:30. Did this also change the diet of animal life? What was their previous diet?

_____

Read Genesis 8:21. What promise did God make about every living creature?

_____

4. Restored earth. Read Acts 3:21.

How long must Jesus remain in heaven? Until it's time to _____ everything.

Read Romans 8:21.

_____ will join God's children in freedom from _____ and decay.

Read Matthew 19:28. What is the "renewal of all things"?

_____

Read Matthew 5:5. Could this mean that evil people are removed and the godly inherit a restored earth?

_____

5. New Earth. Read Isaiah 65:17-25. What will the wonderful new earth make you forget (17)?

_____

What city of joy will be part of new earth (verse 18)?

_____

What will ultimately be heard no more in that city (verse 19)?

_____

What will life spans be like in that city (verse 20-23)?

_____

What changes in the habits of animal life will be evident there (verse 25)?

_____

Read Isaiah 66:1. What two items illustrate the proximity of heaven to earth?

_____

What does this reveal about the proximity of heaven to earth and their ties to each other?

_____

Read Isaiah 66:12-24. It will be a place of _____.

What will happen to the wealth of the nations?

_____

Read Isaiah 66:15-16. What accompanies the coming of the Lord?

_____

Read Isaiah 66:18. Who will come see God's glory there?

_____

Read Isaiah 66:22. How long will new earth last?

_____

Read 2 Peter 3:3-4. What will unbelievers say about the second coming and the eternal kingdom?

_____

Read 2 Peter 3:5. This led to unbelief: they refused to acknowledge God as _____, and chose instead to believe in evolution.

Read 2 Peter 3:7. What will happen to this current post-flood world?

_____

Read 2 Peter 3:8-9. How relevant is "time" to God?

_____

Read 2 Peter 3:10-13. Describe the day of the Lord's judgment:

_____

_____

_____

_____

What will ultimately replace the current earth?

_____

Read Revelation 21. Here (and in chapter 22) we have great detail about new earth.

Describe the oceans on new earth (verse 1):

_____

Describe the capital city (verse 2):

_____

Where will God ultimately live (verse 3)?

_____

What will God do about our tears (verse 4)?

_____

Does this mean there will actually be some temporary sadness in heaven?

_____

What does this say about our memories in eternity?

_____

What does God plan to do—restore everything, or replace everything (verse 5a)?

_____

Can we bank on this (verse 5b)?

Will there be water there (verse 6)?

Who will get to be there (verse 7-8)?

Where will the capital city come from (verse 9)?

Describe the capital city (verses 10-14):

What is the light source to new earth and its capital city (verses 23-25)?

Read Genesis 2:9. Was the tree of knowledge a real tree with real fruit? Explain:

If you said, "No, it's merely a symbol for evil." Answer the next question. If you said, "Yes," then skip the next question.

Did Adam and Eve get kicked out of the garden of Eden for eating imaginary fruit?

_____

Read Genesis 2:9 again. Was the tree of life a real tree with real fruit? These two trees in the garden of Eden are in the same chapter—even in the same verse. Explain:

_____

_____

_____

_____

_____

If the tree of life in Genesis was a real tree with real fruit (and I think it is), is it just as real in the book of Revelation? If not, why not? Explain:

_____

_____

_____

_____

_____

Read Revelation 22, the last chapter in the Bible. Describe the river (verse 1-2):

_____

_____

_____

Describe the tree of life (verses 1-2):

What will be of the curse God placed because of sin (verse 3-5)?

Describe the relationship on new earth between God and people (verses 3-4):

Does this seem similar to that same relationship in the garden of Eden? Explain:

What is the light source for new earth (verse 5)?

_____

Scripture promises the saved will reign with Christ. How long will that last (verse 5)?

_____

Read Revelation 5:10. Where will that be?

_____

Read Revelation 22:12. The Lord is bringing our rewards when He comes. How will these rewards be distributed in terms of proportions for each individual? Explain:

_____

_____

_____

_____

_____

Who ultimately has the right to the tree of life (verse 14)?

_____

_____

_____

_____

_____

Read Revelation 7:9-14. What does the wearing of white robes signify in Scripture? Explain:

_____

_____

_____

_____

Read Revelation 22:15. Who has been removed (from new earth)?

_____
_____
_____
_____

Read Revelation 22:17. What is the cost of the water from the river of life?

_____
_____
_____
_____

The book of Revelation is a book of _____ (verse 18).

Read Revelation 1:3. What happens to people who read the book of Revelation?

_____
_____
_____
_____

Read Revelation 22:18-19. What happens if you change the message of the book of Revelation?

_____
_____
_____
_____

Read Psalm 37:27-29. How long will the righteous live in the land?

_____

Read Isaiah 11:9. Ultimately, who on earth will know the Lord?

_____

Read Isaiah 24:23. Ultimately, where will the Lord reign?

_____

Read Isaiah 40:10. What is the Lord bringing with Him when He comes?

_____

Read Matthew 8:11. What will one of the most delightful activities in the kingdom?

_____

Read Hebrews 1:2. What all will Jesus inherit?

_____

_____

Where or What Is Heaven?

Many verses about God and heaven show a connection to the clouds.

Read Exodus 19:9. Where was God when He approached Moses?

_____

Read Acts 1:9. How were clouds involved in the ascension of Jesus?

_____

Read Daniel 7:13-14. How will clouds be involved in the second coming?

_____

What will Jesus have authority over at that time (verse 14)?

_____

How long will that kingdom and authority last (verse 14)?

_____

Read Amos 3:7. What all does God reveal to His prophets? Just our past, or does it include our future? If not, why not? What is left out? Explain:

_____

_____

_____

_____

_____

Read Matthew 17:2-5. How was a cloud involved in the transfiguration?

_____

_____

_____

_____

_____

_____

Read Matthew 24:1. What did the disciples want Jesus to notice?

_____

Read Matthew 24:2. How did Jesus respond to this?

_____

Read Matthew 24:3. How many questions did the disciples as Jesus?

_____

They thought this was just one question because they thought if the temple (the place where God lived) was destroyed it would be the end of the world. It was actually two questions:

1. "Lord, when will this happen?" (When not one stone will be left upon another.)
2. "Lord, what will signal your return and the end of the world?"
The answer to question one was AD 70 when Rome sacked Jerusalem, when many were killed.
The answer to question two was a long list of events.

Read Matthew 24:21. How will this time of anguish differ from all other historical events?

_____

Read Matthew 24:22. What is at stake unless God intervenes?

_____

Read Matthew 24:24. What will happen to the sun and moon?

_____

Read Matthew 24:29. What will happen to the evil powers in the unseen?

_____

_____

God, His Creation, and Clouds

Read Psalm 104:1-3. How does God move around earth?

_____

Read verse 5. How firm are the foundations of earth?

_____

Read verse 24. Who owns all the creatures of earth?

_____

Read verse 31. God will endure _____ and rejoice in all His _____.

Read verse 35. What will happen to the sinners on earth?

_____

MY SEARCH FOR THE REAL HEAVEN WORKBOOK

When who will be left, and where will they be?

Read Psalm 68:33-34. Where does God's voice originate?

Read Psalm 18:9-15. Where does God come down from (verse 9)?

What were under His feet as He descended (verse 9)?

What does He soar on (verse 10)?

What hides Him in the sky (verse 11-12)?

Where does the Lord attack His enemies from (verse 13-15)?

Learning a Lesson from the Fig Tree

Read Hosea 9:10. What does the fig tree often symbolize?

Read Matthew 24:30-34. What is the lesson of the fig tree (verse 32)? What generation will not all pass away before the second coming (verse 34)? If the fig tree represents Israel, and a fig tree blossoming represents Jews recognizing Jesus as Messiah, this has happened from about 1960 to the year 2000. There are now many Messianic Jews all over the world. We are the generation that has witnessed this phenomenon. So perhaps we are the generation that will witness the second coming (From *The Fig Tree Blossoms*, by Paul Liberman).

Here's the bottom line. There are roughly 120 Old Testament prophecies—all literal—that prove Jesus is the Messiah. There are over 300 New Testament prophecies yet to be fulfilled. These many unfulfilled second coming prophecies are mixed in with the literally fulfilled first coming ones. It's all very confusing, and Isaiah

9 is a perfect example. Christians point to the names of Jesus—"Wonderful Counselor, Mighty God, Prince of Peace,"—and see fulfillment. But Jews point to the intermingled unfulfilled sections like, the government resting on Messiah's shoulders, death removed, and all sickness and disease ending. Read Isaiah 9. Verse 1 talks about no more gloom or distress, verses 5 discusses that every item of war will be burned, verse 6 tells that the government will rest on his shoulders, and verse 7 says that government will originate from David's throne—and is unending! Then verse 18 says all wickedness will be burned in a fire, and verse 19 added that evil people will be added to it.

What's the answer? Again, there are two comings, not just one. He came once as a suffering servant, and will return as a ruling King. Never forget it. Never doubt it.

The Merging of Heaven and Earth

Read Revelation 5:13. Who cheers for God as He sits on His throne?

_____

Why does it say every "creature" instead of every person?

_____

How long does every single creature praise God on His throne?

_____

Explain the length of "forever":

_____

Could this mean a merging of heaven and earth for eternity? Why, or why not? Explain:

_____

_____

_____

_____

Premise: Heaven Is Wherever God Is

Do you agree or disagree that heaven is wherever God is? Explain why/why not:

_____

_____

_____

If you agree with this statement, then was the original, perfect earth—where God walked with man in the cool of the day—originally a part of heaven? Why or why not? Explain:

_____

_____

_____

_____

_____

If the original earth really was a part of heaven—effectively "heaven on earth"—then what had to happen once sin occurred? Select all correct answers:

- ☐ The borders of heaven had to be temporarily redrawn because a holy God cannot come into contact with a cursed planet.
- ☐ After sin, and after God separated Himself from mankind, every time He appears in Scripture from then on—there is fire.
- ☐ God had to put an angel with a flaming sword between mankind and the tree of life.

Read Romans 8:19-23. Does this mean all creation will be restored? Why or why not? Explain:

_____

_____

_____

_____

Thought question: If heaven is wherever God is, if the original earth was part of heaven, and if God plans to restore everything, then could this effectively mean the remerging of the dimensions of heaven and earth for eternity? Why or why not? Explain and discuss:

_____

_____

_____

_____

Read Genesis 8:21 and Revelation 22:3-5. See if you agree with this sequence:
   Original earth was perfect and part of heaven, since God was there.
   Sin required that God place a curse on every molecule of creation.
   God has grand plans for resurrection and restoration.
   At the resurrection, the godly will be reanimated then transformed into immortals.
   Jesus comes back, bringing our rewards and all the godly dead with Him.
   Jesus rules from David's throne.
   Death is the last enemy Jesus will remove.
   Christians are granted positions based on faithfulness, ruling with Christ.
   God will be present, providing light for all (the restored) creation.
   We live forever with Him.

Review

Read pages 194-198 in book

What Might Be: The Hall of Pictoglyphs

Discussion Questions

1. Is it really possible God will save items special to us for eternal enjoyment?

2. Might there really be actual trees in heaven?

3. Might there really be wonderful, fragrant flowers in heaven?

4. Could it be that colors and smells are richer and fuller in heaven?

5. Who are image-bearers? Whose image do they bear?

6. Will we really experience joy at the reminders of pleasant memories from the past?

7. Won't heaven mainly be focused on an exciting future rather than the past?

8. Who were the giant beings with swords in the enhanced pictures?

9. What were these giants watching for and guarding against?

10. Does this really happen in the unseen right now?

Chapter 7: God Promotes a Reward System

Read John 12:26. What will God do for all those who serve Him?

_____

Life is all about rewards. We are rewarded for a paycheck, a diploma, promotions, and raises. Some think going for a reward from God is selfish, that heaven was socialistically equal for all, but that doesn't match Scripture.

Read Matthew 25:21 and 23. What will faithful servants be put in charge of?

_____

Read Luke 19:12-19. What type of leadership position was offered to these faithful servants?

_____

Was it an equal position for each faithful servant?

_____

Wouldn't unequal gifts lead to jealousy and strife? Explain:

_____

_____

_____

_____

_____

_____

Read 1 Corinthians 6:3. Who will the godly judge in heaven?

_____

Read Ephesians 6:8. What is tied directly to each reward given?

_____

Read Romans 2:6. What in this passage is tied directly to each reward given?

_____

Read Luke 6:22-23. What in this passage is tied directly to each reward given?

_____

Read Luke 14:13-14. What in this passage is tied directly to each reward given?

_____

Read Matthew 19:21. What could you do that could make you perfect in God's eyes?

_____

Is everyone expected to do this? Does everyone have the same calling? Why or why not?

_____

Read Matthew 10:42. Will there be eternal reward even for very small things we do?

_____

Read Malachi 3:16. Are things being recorded on scrolls in heaven? Explain:

_____

_____

_____

_____

That's where I want to be: a place of rest, relief, and learning.

Read 1 Corinthians 9:24-27. Who all can win the prize on the race to heaven?

_____

How long will heavenly prizes last?

_____

Does occasional random effort work, or does it require a focused, prolonged one?

_____

Will it be worth it? Explain:

_____

One you commit to God and obey Him, are you safe or still at risk of missing out? Explain:

_____
_____
_____
_____
_____

God Promotes a Reward Economy

Read Genesis 15:1. Who brought up the idea of a reward?

_____

Read 1 Samuel 17:27. Was David interested in a reward for killing Goliath?

_____

Read 1 Samuel 26:22-23. What does this passage say that God rewards?

_____

Read Psalm 37:18. How long do God's rewards last?

_____

Read Psalm 94:15. Who gets God's rewards?

_____

Read Isaiah 3:10. How will it be for the righteous?

_____

Read Isaiah 40:10. Will we "go" to get our rewards, or will they be brought here? Explain?

_____

Read Isaiah 49:4. Where are your rewards right now?

_____

Read Isaiah 61:8. God will reward and make an eternal _____ with them.

Read Isaiah 62:11. Jesus is _____ and bringing our _____ with Him.

Read Ephesians 2:8-9. Salvation is a __ __ __ __, but rewards are __ __ __ __ __ __.

Read Revelation 19:7-8. Rewards begin with a wedding __ __ __ __ __.

Read Jeremiah 32:19. Circle the right answer: according to a) equality, or b) deeds.

Read Matthew 5:11-12. The reward will be __ __ __ __ __.

Read Matthew 6:1-6. What happens to your reward if you do something good just to be seen?

_____

What happens to your reward if you pray just to be seen?

_____

Read Matthew 6:16-18. What happens to your reward if you fast just to be seen?

_____

Who always knows if you do the right thing for the wrong reason? _____

Read Matthew 10:41. Does this seem to say that rewards are unique for each person?

_____

Read Matthew 24:45-46. How will it be for the Master to return and find you faithful?

_____

Read Luke 6:22-23. What does it do for your heavenly reward when people persecute you?

_____

God's rewards are specific and appropriate to the deed. Everyone's deeds are different; therefore, every reward is different:

Read Luke 6:35. What does it do for your heavenly reward when you are kind to your enemies?

_____

Read Luke 14:14. When will you receive your rewards from God?

_____

Read Luke 16:9. How does it help you in eternity when you use earthly resources to help others?

_____

Read Luke 19:15-19. How is eternal position linked to your earthly use of your resources?

_____

Read 1 Corinthians 3:13-15. When your motivation is wrong, what happens to your rewards?

_____

Read Ephesians 6:8. Are slaves exempt from receiving rewards? _____

Read Philippians 4:1. How can one person be a "reward" for another?

_____

_____

_____

_____

Read Matthew 6:19-20. Is this a command, or a suggestion? _____

What happens to treasures stored here?

_____

Isn't it selfish to store up treasures for ourselves? Why or why not? Explain:

Where are we told to store our treasures? Why? Explain:

Read 1 Timothy 4:8. How does training ourselves in godliness affect us? Explain:

Read Hebrews 10:35. What will be the ultimate result for faithful, confident Christians?

Read Hebrews 11:24-26. Compare the time length of sin's pleasures to heaven's rewards.

_____

_____

_____

_____

_____

Read 1 Peter 1:17. Describe how God judges the deeds of each person.

_____

Read 1 Peter 5:4. When you get your crown from God, how long will it last?

_____

Read 2 John 1:8. Is it possible to lose your rewards or get less than you would have? How?

_____

Read Revelation 22:12. When Jesus comes back, what will He bring with Him?

_____

What will be the basis of how He presents rewards?

_____

Review

Read pages 218-222 in book

What Might Be: a Place in the Capital City

Discussion Questions

1. This scene opens with what appears to be Jamie and the angel just appearing in a new place. Are there any examples of this in the Bible? (Read Acts 89:26-40 and John 20:19-28 and discuss.)

2. Might there really be paintings and furniture in heaven?

3. Might we really have angel servants in heaven? (Read Hebrews 1:14 and discuss.)

4. Will there really be parties, banquets, and celebrations in heaven? Discuss.

5. Will there really be mountains, valleys, streams, and rivers in eternity?

6. Did God really promise us a room in His house?

7. Is baptism really part of a covenant relationship with God? How?

8. Might there really be gifts from God with memories attached to them?

9. I thought there wouldn't be any tears in heaven. What about tears of joy?

Chapter 8: Reunion

Read 2 Timothy 1:4. Do you think our heavenly reunion will include tears? Explain:

_____

Instant Gratification: Today's Mantra

The world today is focused on instant gratification. The world wants what it wants—now. The King has a different plan: work hard a little while—seventy or eighty years of life—and enjoy heaven forever. Most have said "no" to this offer. We prefer to trade in a $10 billion inheritance —that's $10,000,000,000—for a $100 per week allowance. Are you making that mistake?

Heaven-Centered Thinking

It has brought me confidence. Once I realized God's pattern of prophetic fulfillment was literal, I grew confident that His promises about eternity are also real and literal. List the ways you are more confident in God's word now that you have explored this idea:

_____

_____

_____

_____

It has increased my faith. God has a plan, and I trust Him to follow through. List the ways your faith is now stronger:

_____

_____

_____

_____

It has brought me excitement about what God has planned for our eternal future. List the things you are more excited about:

___

It has encouraged me evangelism. I am excited about heaven, and I suddenly want to take others with me. List some people you now realize you need to focus on, pray for, and encourage toward heaven:

___

It has enhanced my prayer life. Prayer is a great—but often unused—method of evangelism. If we pray for circumstances to occur in the lives of others that cause them to realize their need for a Savior, there's nothing they can do—they are completely defenseless against our prayers. State your own new, personal commitment to prayer—and then stand by it:

___

Heavenly Citizenship

Read Hebrews 13:14. What do Christians look forward to? Explain:

_____

_____

_____

_____

_____

_____

How would the meaning have been changed if it had said, "We look forward to being taken to the city"? That would have given this statement a completely different meaning, wouldn't it?

_____

_____

_____

_____

_____

_____

Read Philippians 3:19-21. Where is your citizenship? _____

Consider heaven and eternity and list all your thoughts of how Christians should feel about it:

_____

_____

_____

_____

_____

Kingdom Secrets

Read 1 Corinthians 2:9. Why waste time trying to study heaven when this verse says we can't understand or even imagine it? Explain:

_____

_____

_____

_____

_____

_____

Read 1 Corinthians 2:10. Who can know about heaven? Who reveals it? How? Explain:

_____

_____

_____

_____

_____

_____

Read Acts 2:38. Who has God's Spirit so they can understand more about heaven?

_____

_____

_____

_____

_____

_____

Read 1 Corinthians 2:14-16. Will non-Christians understand things about heaven? Explain:

Read Philippians 1:21-23. Is death actually better for a Christian or not? Explain:

Read Colossians 1:18-20. What is Christ destined to be supreme over? Explain:

What did Christ come to reconcile back to God? Explain?

How does Christ's sacrifice make peace with every*thing*?

What's the difference between everything and everyone?

Plato's Heaven versus Christian Heaven

Plato taught that all flesh was evil by nature; therefore, eternity with God must be only spiritual. Does this conflict with Scripture? Read Genesis 1:31. The original creation was quite tangible. Did God consider it evil, or good? Explain:

Greeting the Coming King

Could it be that the triumphal entry gives us a glimpse of the second coming?

Read John 12:12-13. When the people out to greet Jesus, what did they call Him?

___

They used the word *Hosanna*, which means, "Please come save us now." Did they expect Him to come take them somewhere else unknown to them, or come be their King? Explain:

___

Read 1 Thessalonians 4:15-18. Answer the following questions as you compare these verses:

Will there still be people living when Jesus returns? _____

Where do the godly people meet Jesus? _____

Where does it say the godly people will be forever after that meeting? _____

Some have assumed that when we meet Him in the air we will leave to go somewhere else. Does it actually say that anywhere in this passage? Is it possible we will greet Him in the air (as the people did at the triumphal entry) and then usher Him down into the kingdom? Explain:

___

___

___

___

___

Does this encourage you or discourage you? Explain:

___

___

___

___

___

Read Revelation 17:14. Who will be with Jesus when He comes and we meet him in the air?

_____

Is it possible we will be transformed into immortals as we meet Him in the air? _____

Is it possible that the purification fires will have cleansed the planet and removed all evil and all evil people—including the curse itself? _____

Is it possible the King will restore the planet into a worldwide Eden where he can live with us, walk with us, and have relationship with us forever? _____

Good People Will Inherit the Land Forever

Read Psalm 37 and answer the following questions:

What happens to the evil people (verse 1)?

_____

Who will get the land (verse 9)?

_____

What happens to the evil people (verse 10)?

_____

Who will get the land (verse 11)?

_____

Now that we know the godly get the land as an inheritance, how long do they keep it (verse 18)?

_____

_____

_____

_____

What happens to the evil people (verse 20)?

_____

Where do those who are blessed by the Lord live (verse 22)? _____

Where will you live forever if you turn from all evil (verse 27)? _____

What will the righteous inherit, and how long will they keep it (verse 29)? Explain:

_____

What does the Lord guarantee that the righteous will inherit (verse 34)?_____

We Will Rule With Christ

Read Genesis 1:26-28. Mankind was created to __ __ __ __

What was mankind made to rule over? Explain:

_____

_____

_____

_____

_____

Read 2 Timothy 2:12. Who will we co-rule with? _____

Read Revelation 5:9-10. Where will we rule? _____

Work in Eternity

Read Genesis 2:2. Does God work? _____ Does God rest? _____

Is this a possible indication that we will work in heaven? Why or why not? Explain:

_____

_____

_____

Eating in Heaven

Read Isaiah 25:6-7. Will we actually eat food in heaven? What will that include? Describe:

_____

_____

_____

_____

_____

Recognizing Others in Eternity

Read Matthew 17:1-4. How did Peter know Moses and Elijah?

_____

_____

_____

_____

Needing Water

Read Luke 16:24-28. What did the rich man in hell want from Lazarus?

_____

_____

_____

_____

Does this indicate that this rich man in hell had a body and a tongue?

_____

Does this indicate possibly that both people in heaven and hell will have tangible bodies?

_____

Did he remember his earthly life? Will we? Why or why not? Explain:

_____

_____

_____

_____

Heavenly Clothing

Read Revelation 19:7-8. The church is the bride of Christ. What do these Christians wear in heaven? What does this represent? Explain:

_____

_____

_____

_____

_____

No One Can Stop God's Plan to Do All This

Read Isaiah 46:9-13. Does God know how all this will end? Explain:

_____

_____

_____

_____

_____

Can anyone stop God's plan from unfolding just as He intends? _____

Will he take us to a place of righteousness or bring it here? _____

Review

Read pages 244-245 in book

What Might Be: the Welcome Party

Discussion Questions

1. Could it be that Jesus will still have His scars from the cross in eternity?
2. Is heaven really a place without pressure or anxiety?
3. Is our earthly "death day" actually our eternal "birthday"?
4. Might our ancestors and old friends really be there to greet us into heaven?
5. Might my welcome party into heaven really include my favorite foods from earth?